L.I.F.E.

L.I.F.E.

A Collection of Poetry

Desiree Castillo

Xulon Press

Xulon Press
555 Winderley Pl, Suite 225
Maitland, FL 32751
407.339.4217
www.xulonpress.com

© 2024 by Desiree Castillo

All rights reserved solely by the author. The author guarantees all contents are original and do not infringe upon the legal rights of any other person or work. No part of this book may be reproduced in any form without the permission of the author.

Due to the changing nature of the Internet, if there are any web addresses, links, or URLs included in this manuscript, these may have been altered and may no longer be accessible. The views and opinions shared in this book belong solely to the author and do not necessarily reflect those of the publisher. The publisher therefore disclaims responsibility for the views or opinions expressed within the work.

Paperback ISBN-13: 978-1-66289-347-6
Ebook ISBN-13: 978-1-66289-348-3

Dedication

This collection of poetry is dedicated to the reader. My hope is that the footprints of my life help you to see the beautiful truth and light that lies before you and walks beside you through this journey of life. My prayer is that you surrender to Him as I did. I also dedicate this book to my Lord and Savior Jesus Christ. Regardless of the countless mistakes I made and no matter how many times I ran away from You and denied You, You never stopped pursuing me. I love You so much for that. I have never experienced love like Yours. Thank you! I will see You soon.

Acknowledgements

I would like to acknowledge my husband, Jonathan. You mean the world to me. Thank you for all your love, support, and fierce prayers. Your encouraging words mean so much to me. I am in awe with what I am witnessing; the Lord is molding you into a warrior. I know He has a great calling upon your life. Thank you for holding down the fort with the family while I fulfill my calling to share my story with the world through this book.

I would also like to acknowledge my daughter Angelina. We have been through so much together, but the Lord has kept you in the palm of His hands. He has watched over you and protected you since He knitted you in my womb. I also know God has a great calling for your life.

Lastly, I acknowledge the smallest and newest member of my family: my daughter Cataleya. If it wasn't for all the sleepless nights when you were born, I probably would not have spent so much time with the Lord all those hours of the night. Because of this, I got closer to Him. Thank you for that. My hope is that you and your sister will learn from my life by reading this book and surrender to this love that I encountered.

I love you all. You all mean so much to me. I am excited to see what the Lord is going to do through this family. Let's fight the good fight until His return, which is very soon.

Content Caution: In this collection, some poetry depicts contents of suicide, physical abuse, sexual abuse, depression, and drug use.

Table of Contents

1. Live Again 1
2. Pain 2
3. Forward 4
4. Changed 5
5. Survivor 6
6. Backslide 7
7. I Wonder 8
8. Long For 9
9. Where Is She? 10
10. Suicide 11
11. Not Even to My Death 13
12. Whispers 15
13. I Am Silence 17
14. Honesty 19
15. The Pressure 20
16. Disguise 22
17. Explorer 24
18. Daydreams of the Lines 26
19. Goddess of Agony 28
20. Dead 30
21. Just Let it End 32
22. Sand and Water 34
23. One Night with You 36
24. Amnesia 38

25. I See, I Hear. 40
26. Twisted 42
27. I'm Speaking to You 44
28. Was 47
29. Why Do You Hurt Me? 49
30. I Did Not Comprehend 51
31. Stop 53
32. Demonic Temptations 55
33. You Don't Believe Me. 58
34. Got To Remember Me. 60
35. Hoping This Isn't Reality. 62
36. I Own It. Thank You. 64
37. How Wonderful 67
38. Dear Heavenly Father 69
39. I See a Young Woman 71
40. He is God 73
41. My Life 76
42. How Could You Love Me? 79
43. Unforgettable 81
44. Help Me to Remember 82
45. You've Taught Me So Much 83
46. Simply Beauty 85
47. This Will Pass. 87
48. All For a Reason 89
49. Now Is the Time. 91
50. You Gave Me Everything. 93
51. Home With You 95
52. The Lost. 98
53. Seeking You. 100
54. Leaving All for You. 102
55. All I've Ever Wanted 104
56. I Won't Give Up 107
57. To The Unwise 109

58. Slowly Awakening 110
59. My Angelina... 113
60. Dear Mother 115
61. The Night I Met You 117
62. My Image 119
63. I Am Sorry 121
64. You Know... 123
65. Inside.. 125
66. Do You Really Think I Don't Know? 127
67. My Shepherd Comes for Me.................................. 129
68. Show Yourself 131
69. You Came to Me 133
70. Time 134
71. The Most Powerful Thing in The World.................. 136
72. The Wait Is Over 137
73. Father 138
74. See You Again.. 140
75. Not Again 142
76. Silent.. 144
77. Awaken and Repent 145
78. The Body of Christ.. 147
79. Shadows of My Past.. 149
80. You Vs Me 151
81. Does It Really Matter... 154
82. Call To Fight Back 156
83. This Journey.. 158

Live Again

A little star conceived.
Shine bright at night,
My precious life.
The evil is day.
Taking away my prey.
With just prayer and faith.
My crime is no longer condemned.
Surprise! Surprise!
My little star lives again!

August 8, 1998

Pain

It's unimaginable.
My eyes tear blood.
Can't You taste my flood?

It's inconceivable
That while my flesh is silent,
I hear my soul scream.
Wondering, when will I be redeemed?

It seemed to be impossible
How one gets hurt without a touch.
I am so depressed.
Can't You feel it through my flesh?
I beg You, help me!
Isn't this agony enough?

You know I suffer.
I know You see!
Lord God, You have the strength.
So, help me please!

April 8, 1999

Forward

You laugh at my face,
Saying I'm a disgrace,
Holding me down,
So that I can't move around.
You say I'll never make it,
But all I see is your hatred.
Trying to make me believe
That He will never be there for me.
But I still get on my knees
And pray that you will leave me be.
I get up with faith and no longer need to hide.
He tells me that you are the father of lies.
I'll be moving on to high ground.
Finally, I see you beneath me.
Now you're down.
Now you're lower.
While you look up,
To see me moving forward.

April 17, 1999

Changed

She once was lost
In the cries from her eyes.
She once was hidden
In the shadows of your lies.
You have controlled her,
Bringing torment to her name.
She decided to no longer be an object of your game.
She is not what the world is.
She serves another,
Throws away the deceitful cover.
She is new.
No more worshipping two.
Listen because she commands.
I walk through new doors.
I am no longer yours!

April 19, 1999

Survivor

I have gone through unimaginable situations in life.
I have felt too much pain,
But I am proud of myself
That I made it this far in this pathetic game.
No matter what situation I'm in,
I will make it
Because, even though I sin,
My God will give me the strength to win.
It is not easy,
But I know I can manage.
I'll be expecting more tasks,
Even though many put me down and say I won't last.
I used to depend a lot on others
To not leave me on my own,
But I found out the long and hard way
that I'll face life alone.
So, hear me when I say,
I am a survivor!

June 8, 1999

Backslide

My Lord,
I have backslid,
But You were still by my side.
I have turned my back on You,
Yet You still kept me alive.
Whenever I fell,
You still helped me up and kept me well.
You are so good to me.
Even when I slip out of Your grip,
Your love is what I see.
Please forgive me
For all my foolishness.
This world, believe me,
I don't want to be a part of this.
Promise me,
When I blow away like the wind,
Alert me with Your bells.
Keep me away from perishing in Hell.
Heaven is where I want to be led.
With the Scriptures, I want to be fed.
You were the only one that revealed the truth.
You have been with me since my first breath.
And for all this, I love You!

June 12, 1999

I Wonder

I wonder how it feels to have clear blue skies.
I wonder how it feels to walk through no rain.
Who will stop this agony, these cries?
I want to know happiness, all to my name.
But so many difficulties, so many tries.
I want to walk on flat grounds
With no more cuts on my bare feet.
I want to walk through light with pleasant sounds.
I want my heart to be complete.
I want happiness but my own.
Not stolen. Not fake.
Not for short moments of time and not a loan.
It's a shame that all I know is pain.
Happiness is what I've been dying to gain.
I wonder when it will be my time.
I hope and pray,
That soon, someday,
It will all be mine.

October 30, 1999

Long For

Give me happiness to express through words.
Let it be known, let it be heard.
Let me show it to family, friends, and other people.
Give me joy and let it not be deceitful.
Give me tears that don't come from being sad.
Let my cries come from being glad.
Give me calmness from comfort.
Begging, help me make that an effort.
Do You see the stripes, the colors on my back?
Destroy what has done that!
Do You see the gushing blood from my heart?
From the first moment of pain, to stop, I prayed from the start.
Kill, murder my illness.
It makes me depressed and weak.
I am tired of having this sickness.
Till my death, happiness is what I seek.
When will I find it?
Will it be mine?
When will the pain end?
Joy, will You please send?
I don't want to suffer anymore.
Give me what I long for.

November 18, 1999

Where Is She?

I suddenly realize,
I am gone. I am gone.
Where am I?
What have I done? What have I done?
I have vanished, disappeared.
I have been looking,
But I am nowhere near.
I am lost.
Will I be found?
Hoping, searching,
But I am nowhere around.
I need to find myself.
I miss her. I miss her.
Will I find me in such a blur?
I slipped. I slipped.
No longer in my grip.
I left me. I left me.
Did not notice. Did not see.
I don't want to say goodbye.
Don't want to continue living a lie.
Where did I go?
Will I come back to me?
Only God knows.

November 29, 1999

Suicide

Sometimes I feel like I see the line,
But then I think, is it my time?
My depression makes me wonder,
What do I live for?
Me? There should be no more.

I feel that it's the end.
Stop! A message He sends.
I walk to the edge of a cliff,
Trying to jump, but He makes my body stiff.

Light it up, I want to burn,
But still thinking, is it my turn?
Pick it up, it's sharp.
Wanting to stick it in my heart.
Knife to skin.
Why can't I seem to feel a thing?
He makes me numb to press deeper.
Yet You rescue me from being his keeper.

Sniff, swallow.
But He says, *to your grave, you shall not follow.*
Inject, inhale.
But He tells me *you're not taking that step into hell.*

L.I.F.E.

All I do is cry.
I feel I need to die.
Pain is all I know.
If I got to go, I got to go.

November 30, 1999

Not Even to My Death

I think about you by day.
I cry thinking about you at night.
I still can't accept the fact that you went away
Because losing you just wasn't right.

I can't take it that you're not here.
All I do is cry a river of tears.
With you gone, I never felt a greater pain.
My loneliness makes me go insane.

Even though I never met you, I miss you so much.
My belly, I can no longer touch.
You are more precious than diamonds themselves.
I would've given up anything to have you here
Instead of being by myself.

I feel empty; I feel bare.
But one day we will see each other.
I promise; I swear.
But until then,
In my heart you live again.

To turn back, it's too late.
Half of me is gone.
Until I'm deceased, on that date,
I'll never forget what was done.

L.I.F.E.

I will always love you,
Surpassing my last dying breath
Because my love for you is so powerful.
It will go beyond my death.

December 2, 1999

Whispers

I just can't figure out why.
All these whispers won't die.
Shhh. Listen, listen.
In me, they speak within.
Even through silence,
I can hear it.
Words of violence.

Their voices are such horrible noises,
Persuading me to make diabolical choices.
The way it sounds is so vicious.
You can tell that it's treacherous.
Too horrifying, I just can't explain.
Praying that soon,
There'll be a change.

When they speak,
All I ask is for a helping hand.
But why isn't it You that I hear?
That I can't understand.
Make it leave.
I beg You, I plead.

L.I.F.E.

Make it disappear.
Vanish all my fears.
I'm scared,
And I know that You are aware.
It's just not fair.

December 26, 1999

I am Silence

Why can't I reach you?
Am I on mute?
What is it that I must do?
Do you have ears?
Do I speak another language
Because it seems to me that you can't hear.

Am I not noticeable?
Am I capable
Of getting you to hear what I have to say
Without you turning the other way?
What the hell am I?
Am I not meaningful?
No matter how hard I try,
To you, I seem pitiful.
I want to be heard so badly.
But my voice makes you deaf.
And that's what makes me unhappy.

I'm tired of being alone.
I want you to give me your attention.
Let my words not be a rejection.
Why do you pay me no mind?
Can you spare some time?
How much will it take

L.I.F.E.

Just to converse?
How can I make
You listen to my words?
Hear me.
Make me known to them, Lord.
Please.

December 30, 1999

Honesty

All I ask is for you to keep it real.
All I want is for you to tell me how you feel.
I don't understand why you lie.
And then when I confront you,
You start to deny.
Why can't you just tell me the truth?
And when you don't, you start to make excuses
When I show you the proof.
Why do I have to hear it from someone else
When you should've told me yourself?
You hurt me a lot.
And don't act like you were going to tell me,
But you forgot.
You need to stop lying and get out of my face.
Your fear of getting caught is what I can taste.
Being a liar
Is what I don't appreciate.
Increasing my anger higher,
Is what I truly hate.
Why don't you just stop all your lies?
For a change, tell the truth,
And give it a try.

January 2, 2000

Showing me how to get through.
Telling me not to be a fool.
Telling me what to say.
Showing me what's the right way.

Telling me to make the right choices,
So, I don't have negative effects.
Always having to hear these voices
Telling me life is so hectic.

This is something I can't escape.
I have no choice but to tolerate.
I feel like I am in a cage.
And then they wonder why
I break out into a rage.

I can't stand all the stress.
Saying you do it for the best.
Always telling me how life gets.
Redundancy only makes it worse.
Your lack of faith in me really hurts.

The pressure is everywhere.
To challenge is the dare.
Because of this,

Desiree Castillo

I feel I need to get away.
Because sometimes I think,
I have no courage to stay.

Pressure, I cannot take it.
Only with God, I can make it.
I don't need your help.
All I need is God and myself.
So please, leave me alone.
I will face life with Him
And on my own.

January 9, 2000

I have a lot of weight on my shoulders.
A lot on my mind.
If I can get this off me for sure,
I wouldn't have to wear a mask all the time.

I use this almost every day
To not show my true emotions.
But people think I'm okay,
Because they don't know about my commotion.

It seems to me I'm always hidden.
All my distress is within.
People see me when I'm smiling,
But truthfully, my impressions are lying.

Every day it feels like Halloween.
But I'm dying to be sincerely seen.
I'm tired of walking around in a costume.
I would love to take it off,
Hoping it will be very soon.

Almighty,
Take away my problems.
Help me to solve them.
Help me to be patient,

And wait for these situations
To stop piling up one after the other.
Especially to no longer have a cover.
Due to my hate, I will wait
For this mask to no longer last.

January 27, 2000

Explorer

I take all chances.
Doing almost anything I please.
Not even bothering to take glances
At other people's experiences.
People think that everyone turns out
With the same consequences.
But I'm willing to investigate about.
Curiosity will reveal the truth.

I take many risks
Because I love the challenge.
Most of the time I'm convinced
That I'll most likely win.
I like to take that test
That life gives us.
And it's obvious I passed
Because I'm living till this day with the help of Jesus.

I do it to find answers.
A lot of people don't do what I do
Because they're scared of what they'll go through.
They don't have faith.
It's themselves that they hate
For not exploring.
So, they still have no answers to their questions.
Their lives must be boring.

Desiree Castillo

I will not let life pass me by.
I refuse to look back
And say I should've tried.
Why haven't I done that?
Even though some of my doings will be wrong,
I will survive because I am strong.
So, don't try to stop me.
Just let me be.
I will just shrug my shoulders.
I was born to be an explorer.

January 29, 2000

Daydreams of the Lines

Sometimes I fiend.
Then I begin to dream.
It's like a ghost.
It haunts,
Making me think I need it most.
And now regretting I chose to want.

When it enters my body,
The pleasure makes me think.
This is not naughty.
Taking it in, one by one.
I open the door.
Allowing demons to come.
Feeling good. Then taking more.

Slowly killing myself.
And at the same time, wishing for help.
Falling, losing my balance.
Throwing away my gifted talents.
Finding blood on my fingers.
But stupid me, why do I linger?
I haven't done it much.
But that next step to death,
All it takes is one touch.

But now I grab the phone.
He has been waiting for this
While sitting on His throne.
I gave Him a ring.
Contacting the King.
He's sitting in Heaven.
Never busy, available 24-7.
He knows what goes on in my mind.
And He will rescue me
From the daydreams of the lines.

January 31, 2000

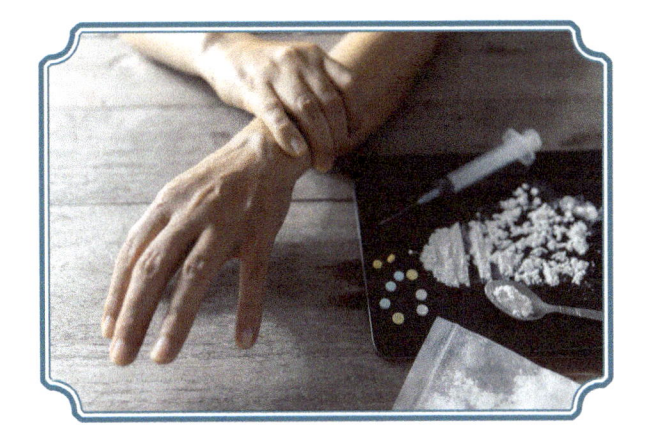

Goddess of Agony

If you ask me,
How does it feel to be happy?
I would feel so ashamed
And tell you that you came
To the wrong person
Because, for certain,
I don't know what that is.

I don't know how it feels.
I don't even know if it is real.
I've never been its owner.
When it comes to that,
I've always been a loner.
I don't know its definition,
But it is my mission
To have, hold, and know.

All I know is agony.
My knowledge is all about misery.
I know all about it.
It's the only thing I've ever lived with.
I'm the goddess of pain.
So used to it, my flesh is calm to the chaos.
So, what's the point of going insane

Desiree Castillo

With this? I'm highly educated,
But believe me, I truly hate it.
It just won't let go of me.
Sewed throughout my body.
If you want me to define
The opposite of being happy,
Then come to the goddess of agony.

February 5, 2000

Dead

I messed my life up.
I can't take it anymore.
Yes, I did it to myself, true enough.
But what do I keep doing it for?

My stupidity gets me nowhere.
My attitude shows I don't care.
I'm mean, dirty, and my choices are dumb.
Not then, but now, I see what I have become.
All I have is ridiculous hate
Because suddenly, I lost my faith.
I've lost everything I had.
My life is so depressing and sad.

It's just all about the drugs.
If I don't get it, I hold a grudge.
It's all about the alcohol.
I'm just getting sicker; my addiction stands tall.
My hobby is to hate.
My question is,
To change, is it too late?
I'm a nasty, disgusting whore.
Help me Almighty!
Please help me, Lord!

I've lost everything, everyone.
I lost me.
I lost touch with the Son.
Continuously hurting my body.
There is no more to be said
Because I feel as if I am dead.

February 25, 2000

Just Let It End

God Almighty.
It's just getting worse by the day.
Everything is falling out of place.
Rivers are still being formed.
Covers of sin are still being worn.
It just won't stop.
Goes on all the time.
People just will not
End all the crime.

Tired of carrying unbearable pain.
So grand that they don't know.
It hangs on us, going wherever we go.
People suffer because of the deadly tongue
Yet are still not prepared for the One who will come.
Every day, blood is shed.
Your return is what I await.
This is what You promised, what You said.

I can't take it anymore.
My heart is completely torn.
I want to be saved
And leave with the most precious gift ever gave.
This pathetic world must be gone.
We must get off this roller coaster,

Desiree Castillo

This twisted life that rides on.
Finish it! This is torture.
Drown our knowledge of pain into a pond.

It must leave.
Stop the breathing.
The bruises itself say please.
Don't You hear it screaming?
The world is a big room.
I'll wait.
I hope You come soon.
Please don't come late.
Please attend.
Just let it end.

February 26, 2000

Sand and Water

Lying on the sand.
Feeling hot and sweaty.
This is what I can't stand,
But the water flows up steadily.
Feeling sensation while it runs rapidly through,
But it was only a moment, just as I knew.
The water rushes back down and away.
While hot and sweaty again,
My agony comes back as I lay.

My pain is the sand
That burns my body and hands.
The water blissfully cools me.
It comes with a beautiful breeze.
My God will make the sand slip away
From the crack of my toes and fingers.
And the happiness I pray
Will be a regulation to bring her.

The water is creeping up slowly.
I feel it; I sense.
It's coming to clean and change me.
My miseries will hence.
It's coming.
My happiness will come and grow.
My pain will shatter with a great blow.

Desiree Castillo

The power of the sand is getting weak.
The ocean waves will hit hard to defeat.
Now is the time to change.
My fierce intentions are no longer the same.

March 23, 2000

One Night with You

He only gave us one night, just one night.
It was amazing how, for one moment in my life,
Everything felt perfectly right.
It was in the future but with a different past.
Oh, Father God, but why couldn't it last?

To touch you felt so good that it hurt.
I had a million things to say,
But there wasn't enough time to say any words.
I held you in my arms,
For just a short moment of time.
What was done, I forgot about that harm.
If it wasn't done, it would've made you mine.
To hear you laugh
Was so beautiful.
For once, I wasn't sad.
About that, I was always doubtful.

I didn't want to let you go.
I was hoping that the time would go by very slow.
To see you smile
Made the time beyond worthwhile.
I've never seen such beauty in my life.
I will never forget your presence in my sight.
Till the day I die, there will be a reminiscence.
That night, your image was burned in my remembrance.

Thank you so much, Father.
I finally held her.
For just that one moment,
My body and soul recovered.
I felt no torment to me.
My cuts and bruises were gone from beating myself physically.
I finally stopped screaming.
For once in my life, I didn't know what pain was or misery.
Since I got to hold my daughter,
I no longer held the title "goddess of agony."

March 27, 2000

Amnesia

Brain damage.
I'm waiting.
I can't know it any longer
Because I'm hating.
I want injury
To no longer know agony.
I will soon have to be taught to be sad.
I will not have the pain that I had.

No more self-pity.
Calm down, insanity.
It will be a law
To stop the madness.
I will have memory loss
Because it's not for me to handle this.
Let me be sick.
I won't know how to be psychotic.
I just can't stand living in chaos.

I won't see blood.
Finally, it's enough.
Where are the cuts and bruises?
They will no longer abuse me.
No more aches.
This damage won't be a mistake.

Desiree Castillo

How do you be stressful?
How do you be pitiful?
I will look this up in the dictionary
Since I won't know hurt or misery.
What is depression?
All this will soon be a question.

I will have this healthy disease.
Damage, I will receive.
Ruin this knowledge in my brain.
I will soon say farewell to pain.

April 10, 2000

I See, I Hear.

Do you see Him?
Yes, I do.
Where do you see Him?
I see Him when I see the night sky
Watch the world with its diamond eyes.
Or when I see the sun rise and set.
When I see the moon wake up from its bed.
When streams are in a race to get to the ocean.
When the trees give their donation.
When I see the intricate design of a mountain.
In all of creation is where He abounds in.
There is no way I can deny
The canvas that is before my eyes.
It all points to Him.

Do you hear Him?
Of course, I do.
When do you hear Him?
I hear Him when the wind howls.
In the movement of animals when they're on the go.
I hear Him when the thunder roars.
When the crashing waves of the ocean go back and forth.
I hear Him in the choir of the forest.
I hear Him in everything before I lay myself to rest.

Desiree Castillo

When I see all this,
I see Him.
When I hear all this,
I hear Him.
I see, I feel His power.
His strength is like an undestroyable tower.
I see, I feel His glory.
He lets me know not to worry.
The beauty He has is natural, sovereign, holy.
Oh Lord, how I love to stand before Your glory!

April 18, 2000

Twisted

No matter what I do,
No matter where I go,
I get madder at you
Because you won't leave me alone.

I thought breathing was about going away.
But there is always a mouth
That has something to say.

Oh, Lord, help me!
Don't hear my cries,
Drink it from my eyes.
Don't look at my cuts,
Smell my perfume of blood.
Don't listen to my scream,
Bathe in it as if it were a stream.

There are laughs behind it.
There is a voice that repeats.
Got this trick!
Flesh and blood think I'm psychotic.
As if they know how it feels to be picked.
They're wrong! You know what I'm talking about.
Show me the exit of this maze.
Show me the way out!

Desiree Castillo

When will I rise from the dead?
When will I get amnesia in my head?
When will I breathe?
When will the demons leave?
When will I know love?
When will my answers come from above?
Can you, reader, relate to me?
Or are you one of those that stupidly thinks I'm crazy?

April 21, 2000

I'm Speaking to You

Yes, you.
I'm talking to you.
You're the one that slithers on the ground.
The one with poison dripping from your teeth.
You're the one that comes from way down.
That is quick, vicious, and sleek.
You capture defenseless prey.
Blood around your mouth.
You're the one that betrays
The people who think there is no way out.

You come to me so much
That I can sit and converse with you.
You can never have enough
Of me being with you.
I cannot speak of dancing with the devil.
Nor you getting inside me below the navel.
I cannot reveal to others about this.
You, the king of lies, that plays tricks.
They'll just think I'm a fool.
Yes, you.
I'm talking to you.

Deceitful, loving words.
You whisper to me.

You wrap your arms around me and say,
You're mine to keep.
You visit me every night
And greet me in different ways.
You change yourself so that I may not recognize,
Especially your face.
You're the one with different names.
I allowed you to make me goddess of pain.
How can you hate so much, and you don't know,
And you always physically show.
I don't understand why you do.
Yes, you.
I'm talking to you.

For you, my enemy,
I worked.
And I, stupidly,
Consented you to search.
With you, I dated,
And others I hated.
I slithered with you, the serpent.
Permitted you to not allow me to repent.

The Lord I tried seeking,
But chained to you, I kept on creeping.
You didn't want others to see.
So, you hid.
While you played with me
As if I were a kid.
I can't believe I stayed with you
After all you put me through.
If you don't go back from which you came,
I will scream out His name.

L.I.F.E.

Would you like me to say who?
Yes, you!
I'm intimidating you!

April 28, 2000

WAS

I held up my strength.
I hope it can last,
But he brings back what I don't need
Silently and very fast.

I walked up the stairs.
I didn't seem to care
To look at where I was led to by the steps.
Now I say to myself because I regret,
Going up to get tall.
Just to know that I'd fall.

I got into the car.
Drove to see how far
I can get.
I listened to what he said.
Mindlessly, I allowed his treatment to my tension.
Senselessly, I drove in his direction.
Permitted myself to crash.
He proved I couldn't last.
All done because I went behind the wheel.
Now praying for me to heal.

I lived with Lucifer in Hell.
Thinking he'll lift me because I fell.

L.I.F.E.

I was his wife.
He controlled my life.
I was his whore.
My body, soul, and mind are what he tore.
He hired me to be employed.
He took away my joy.
Abused me is what he did.
All this, I would kill to rid.
Rule me is what he does,
But now ruler is what he was.

May 8, 2000

Why Do You Hurt Me?

Why, mother, why?
Why have you done this to me?
Why was I brought to this world to breathe?
Since I was born,
I have mourned.
Since I can remember,
Your mouth has been sewed shut.
You have not been there for me
While growing up.
You have beaten me in different ways.
Until you made me vision my grave.
All of me would feel so sore
Because I would feel half dead on the floor.

When I bleed,
You do not care to see.
When I have bruises,
Your tongue just speaks refuses.
You just see me as a burden, a chore.
Ashamed of me is the clothes you wore.
You try to buy my love materialistically.
Just so you can hold it against me.
I cannot touch you
Because it is so painful.
I cannot listen to you
Because your voice sounds pitiful.

L.I.F.E.

Do you really think I can trust you?
Did you forget the murder committed that was cruel?
You don't answer any of my calls.
You don't hold me when I fall.
You weren't there for me to lean on.
Will we ever have a bond?
For all this, it is hard for me to forgive you.
After all the things you put me through.

So, don't you see?
I raised me.
For so long,
I taught me right from wrong.
I fought in life by myself.
You were never there when I needed help.

I spend more time with the devil.
Saying you're mine?
I'm just not able!
I hope that someday, you will know who I am.
I hope that someday, you will understand.
May the power of the living God reconcile a true loving relationship between us.

May 12, 2000

I Did Not Comprehend

I did not know how I survived.
I can't believe I am still alive.
How did I make it all alone?
Now I see, I did not let him pass my bones.
Now I realize
That I was so brave.
Finally, I magnified
To see that I am still saved.

A few good things did come out of my agony.
The whole time, Jesus was with me.
The more I was put down,
The more I got stronger.
I allowed no bound,
So, my faith stayed longer.
I fought more and more.
So, I wouldn't have to endure
The thought that I would fail.
So, I proved that I'd prevail.

I can help others
That feel like an outcast.
I would tell them that the
Lord will help them to surpass.
They will not walk down the same road.
I'd motivate them to be wise and bold.

L.I.F.E.

My life is changing.
Stability, I'm gaining.
I put up a lot of fights,
Against the one I despised.

Wow!
I made it somehow!
The answer is Jesus.
He never leaves us.
I'm not the only one that proved something.
I'm beyond amazed.
I made it through all these days.
Jesus really does work in mysterious ways.

May 16, 2000

Stop

Family, family.
Do you see, can't you see?
Do you have any idea of what is going on?
Do you realize what went wrong?
We can't even touch each other.
We can't even look at one another.
We won't even forgive.
Like this, I cannot live.
Don't you realize?
That he has you all hypnotized?
Just stop and think
Before our faith begins to sink.
All we do to each other is fight.
He has taken away our sight.
He is trying to defeat us.
We've all forgotten about Jesus.
To take our souls is his job.
He wants what belongs to God!

Now as for you, Satan!
I have worked with you.
I know what you're up to.
Just once more.
Show your face.
This time,

L.I.F.E.

I have something to say.
Come to me,
And I will do the talking!
Trust me,
I will do the mocking!
Now it is my turn.
I will show you what I've learned.
You are nothing but old news.
You are nothing but the dirt under my shoes.
Get off my property, off my backyard.
You do nothing but break people apart.
Come, I'll tell you and you will see.
What I will do to you will make you extremely afraid of me!

May 18, 2000

Demonic Temptations

It is me again.
Hear my voice?
I am here to lend,
And you have no choice.

Don't come to me to lend,
You aren't my friend.

I am you.
I will rule.

It's no longer you and me.
You? I will defeat.

But we're one.

No, I love His Son.

It is you I want to caress.

You just spoke dishonest words when you addressed.
My eyes are finally open.
Now I realize what is better for me.
Even though I was desperately hoping,
I don't want to engage in your things.

L.I.F.E.

I am the cane that helped you walk.

If anything, it's you I no longer sought.

Wanting the liquid to rush through your veins.
Long hours of being high made you insane.

Hell no, get out of my brain.
Don't want to suffer nor to bane.

Never mind about the blood that rushed.
It was worth it.

I care about those I crushed,
And I won't forget it.
I don't want to abuse.

Doesn't matter.
I'll give you more of what you used.
I'll give you a lover.
I'll give her back to you.

Stop! Bother another!
I only did it because I wanted love. I was desperate.

So come to me; you won't regret it.
Just admit it, you are very much tempted.

Still, I'll not consent to it.

Come, you can't resist that.

No! I won't go back!
If you don't leave,
God will command His angels to attack.
In His name, you must flee!
They will not stop fighting you for me.

June 12, 2000

You Don't Believe Me

You put your foot down
And act so strict
Because you think I play around,
Like if I'm that same old trick.
You really believe
I'm still a drug addict.
You warn me that you'll creep.
Let me guess,
You still think I run the streets.
You don't believe that my judgement is good now
Because you still feel I will mix in with the wrong crowd.
You probably think I still
Pop girls in the face.
Getting you to trust me
Will take so many days.
You think I'll throw money away.
Did you forget that I never had any from where I used to stay?
So how can you say I'll waste it
When I never proved that I would when I never had it to begin with.
I can go on and on.
It's ashame that you see and do wrong.
Sorry to break it down like this,
But I am furious because of your ignorance.
You complain too much about this and that.
There is no trust because of the past.

Desiree Castillo

You don't know because you don't try.
So, you think you know, but it's just a lie.
Why am I so looked down on?
This has been bothering me for so long.
All of you do it to me.
Although your mouth speaks different,
Your actions show it constantly.
I can't just turn away and ignore.
But at the same time, I don't know what to do about it anymore.
How will I get you to believe
That He really did change me?
It hurts me that the ones I love don't see.
If it's going to be this way,
What more can I possibly say?

August 4, 2000

Got To Remember Me

I saw me.
Yes, memories.
Trying to have fun
In all the wrong ways.
Then, looking at what was done,
Why the hell did I do it is what I'd say.
Yeah, that was me.

Getting messed up
Until I'm dragging on the floor.
Bastards taking advantage,
As if I'm a disgusting whore.
Doing stupid things
And thinking that it's cool.
But got to remember, Desirée.
Remember this isn't you.
It's pitiful, it's nasty.
How pathetic to know
That used to be me.

Telling the innocent to throw their hands up.
Telling my people,
Let's get this girl jumped.
Thinking this was right.
Not remembering it was done to me,

I still go ahead and fight.
I should have walked away and just let it be.
Yeah, that was me.

Playing, messing with girl's minds.
Got to remind myself time after time.
I'm not bi-sexual, I'm not gay.
I know what's really behind this.
I know this being.
I've seen this person in that realm.
From its deceit, I must stay away
Or else I will hear it on judgement day.
It's not worth doing and then regret.
Sorry, my love, it's just not me.
Don't want to disrespect.

There is a whole lot more that I didn't want to see.
It is so good to realize the truth,
Because none of this is really me.
Got to praise and serve my savior, my Lord.
That's who I am, and that is what I want to do.
Now always remember,
Yes, this is definitely you!

August 11, 2000

Hoping This Isn't Reality

Death is awakening.
Voices are tormenting.
Death is breathing.
Faith is leaving.
Visions of a body.
I'd rather not know,
But it's sad that I do.
He won't leave me alone.
He told me it was you.

I never had a relationship with you.
I'm starting to think that'll never.
I don't know you.
Seems like death will take its place forever.
Little by little, you disappear.
First your voice,
Then you're not here.

Will it come to a point
Where I must grip flowers,
And then lay it down on that hour.
While you're lying quietly alone,
I'm standing upon that grave.
Staring at the stone.
Staring at the name engraved.

Desiree Castillo

Believe me, I don't want to say goodbye.
Oh why, why did this have to happen?
Sister, please, don't pass me a napkin.
My tears have already gone to waste.
I was told that death would take its place.

Even though our relationship was cruel.
I really do love you.

August 13, 2000

I Own it. Thank you.

What I wanted I did not find, and I looked in all the wrong places.
Running and ended up running into those same laughing faces.
All I wanted was something I never had before.
I wanted to be healed from this disease that I've endured.
I searched and searched and found myself in a pit.
The pain I had, oh, how I tried to get rid of it.
I didn't listen when He whispered,
I can help you climb out of it.
For so many years, I have done things my way
And never cared to hear what He had to say.
But finally, I surrendered, and I said,
Lord, take this pain that I've bestowed upon me before I end up dead!
So, He spoke.

I've had what you wanted.
I've been holding what you hunted.
Do you want a little taste, or will you just let it go to waste?
Come, Desirée, and take what I have.
Believe me, after I am through with you, Satan will be extremely mad.

So, I took a taste of His kind of meal.
And no words can describe what I feel!
It smells, feels, and tastes so good that I just can't explain!
You, reader, will know what I mean by just saying His name!
I felt a quiver.

My whole body shivered.
The burden was so light.
My spirit was finally alive.

All my life, I have wanted happiness.
And finally found the one to stop this madness.
Oh Father, forgive me for not going to you first!
I'm sorry, I truly am.
And He said, *I don't know why you went to the worst,*
but because I love you, I will give you a helping hand.

Now I have what I long for.
But God said, *hold on, I got more!*
Giving me joy, He still isn't done.
He said to me, *Desirée I've only just begun!*
Now I know because I feel it.
And this time I did not have to steal it.

Thank you, Lord. Thank you for what you have given me.
Jesus, You are my Savior.
And He said to me,
No one can resist my flavor!

I am finally free.
You broke the chains off my wrist and ankles.
The demons flee.
Their work is finally dismantled.

August 27, 2000

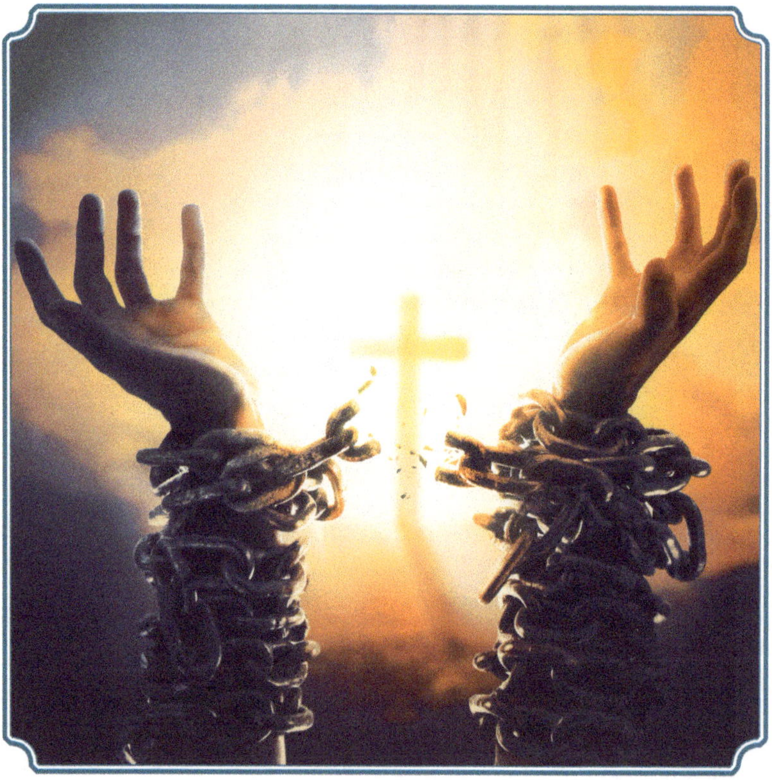

How Wonderful

It happened last night.
You tested me.
It's alright
Because they didn't defeat.
I meant what I said.
I have changed completely.
While I was on that bed,
They came to meet me.
They were bothering so much,
Speaking such deceit.
But I kept my strength up.
I held on to my faith
Because that is something they'll no longer take.
I screamed, I shouted.
I spilled my heart out.
While praising You, I had no doubts.
You waited awhile to see if I'd give up,
But I proved that I wouldn't.
So, You said *enough is enough*.
The angel tapped me on the shoulder and said *it's alright now*.
I was so amazed that I got on my knees and bowed.
I cried, sang, and praised You at one in the morning.
Your presence and glory, on me, was pouring.
Even though my eyes did not see, my heart did.
Only my ears heard the angel and the Lord's voice.

L.I.F.E.

Oh, how I am overjoyed by my choice.
This joy and happiness I never felt before.
Oh, Father God, it's You that I want more and more.
I heard the angels singing all around me.
Singing and worshipping out into the heavens.
Oh, how wonderful it is to be,
No longer in the reach of Satan.
Lord, You are now seated and centered in my heart.
We will never be apart.
You give me such indescribable joy.
I am no longer Satan's toy.
How wonderful it was last night!
Now and forever, You will always be in my life.

August 28, 2000

Dear Heavenly Father

It's amazing what you have done in my life.
I thank You for sending Your Son, Jesus Christ.
You proved to many people that it was not impossible to change this girl.
You continue to mold me every day as I face this world.
You also proved me wrong. I never thought that I could change.
I have waited so long, and now You've finally got rid of the pain.
You do so much for me.
You have kept me to breathe.

I don't deserve any of this.
In all the wrong places, I was trying to find love and happiness.
Thinking that money, drugs, and so on would give me bliss.
I risked my life to get joy that was so fake and pursued it continuously.
While all the time you were trying to tell me
That the joy You give is for all eternity.
The happiness I took was dishonest and only lasted for a moment.
I can't believe after all that I did, You still condoned it.

I was so dark and hollow.
Pain is what I swallowed.
I was cold and dead.
I cry because you took the time to wake me from my coffin bed.
I was the one that loved and was loved by death.
The one that breathed Satan's breath.

I can't believe you.
You showed me that your love and happiness is true.
What You have done in my life is so wonderful.
The love that You have is amazingly powerful.

You took away my evil intentions.
Now I am so happy that we have an intimate connection.
You showed me who the Almighty God is!
I never knew happiness.
I never thought that I could.
Although I always heard about it, I never knew it would feel this good.

Thank you. I love You.
I will worship You, praise You, and do the task that You have given me.
Right before You is exactly where I want to be.

October 6, 2000

I See a Young Woman

I see a little girl.
A girl hoping, seeking.
I see a girl praying, weeping.
Oh, hopeless little girl.
Wondering while beaten.
Will soon be evilly thinking.

I see a girl.
Seeing, knowing too much.
I see a girl with so much pain building up.
A girl so hungry.
Hungry for love and happiness,
Wanting peace and no madness.

I see a girl.
Having to grow quicker than others.
Learning faster than others.
A bleeding girl, all alone.
Doing everything on her own.
How badly she wanted to be held.
You couldn't look at her, nasty, ugly, and pale.

I see a girl losing the only things she had.
A girl screaming, so depressed and so sad.
Doing the unthinkable just to get by.

L.I.F.E.

Then just trying, was so eager to die.
A girl turned so evil, cruel.
How badly she wanted to hurt, kill you.

She made an appointment with her grave.
The girl no longer wanted to stay.
I saw the girl leave with a silent goodbye.

I see a young woman.
Could this be?
The impossible happened.
Should I believe?
The Lord has been watching over her all along.
God is the one that made her strong.
Gave her true love from above.
A young woman now healed.
Overwhelming happiness is what she feels.

No longer alone.
She now has a permanent home.
She cries joy and praises her Father.
The young woman said, *Lord, I am your daughter.*
Little girl but she died.
A young woman.
Just look in her eyes.
I'm alive!

October 11, 2000

He is God

I was alone. No one to speak to. No one to go to.
I was in a hole. I was so depressed, feeling such sorrow.
I wanted to scream but no one would hear me.
The hole got deeper. So deep that there is
No light shining.
I didn't even realize I dug this hole with my own bare hands.
So dark, so silent. I ate dirt and there were worms all over me.
My mouth was so dry that I couldn't scream anymore.
The only thing I drank were the tears pouring down my face.

Something fell on me.
I looked to see and saw that it was a flower.
A flower that turned into a dagger and stabbed me right in the heart.
Then I came to realize that people thought I was dead.
I was a corpse that dug my own grave.
I sank into my coffin of blood, blood that rushed from my bleeding heart.
People didn't care to listen to my cries and help me
yet had the audacity to attend my funeral.
How is it that they cannot see that I was buried alive?
They gave me a tombstone without a name.
How can they forget my own name?
By this point, I would have given anything
To have physical pain than mental pain.
All my life, I have felt all this until now.

L.I.F.E.

I had seen someone come with a shovel in His hands.
He dug me out of my grave and took the dirt that was on top of me away.
He came with a rope so that I could climb out of my deep hole.
He turned towards my tombstone, and He kicked it.
It shattered to the ground.
Then He blew air into my mouth so that I may breathe again.
He gave me life, and from one look in His eyes, He gave me light.
Then He took the knife out of my heart and stitched my wound.
Then He came with a waterfall to wash away
The worms, dirt, and blood that was all over me.

I was fresh and had a wonderful scent.
He gave me a handkerchief to dry up my tears.
He gave me water to drink to stop the dryness in my mouth.
He gave me food to please my tummy.
He came with open arms and welcomed me into His home.
Without me saying a word, He said my name.
How did He know my name?

He told me to get some rest and then He tucked me into bed.
He blew me a kiss and whispered, *good night and I love you.*
I turned and looked at Him. I couldn't believe who I was seeing.
I couldn't believe who came after me.
I couldn't believe what He had done for me.
I couldn't believe He knew me.
He knew my name.
He gives me limitless love, happiness, peace and so much more.
He is God!

October 19, 2000

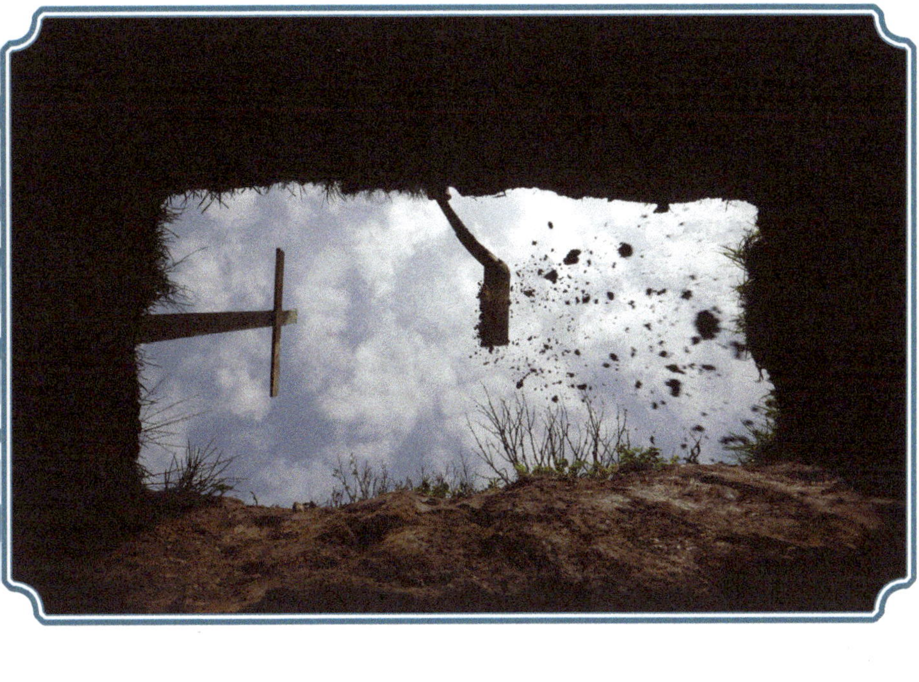

My Life

My life is a perfect example.
It is evidence that God is able.
I honestly didn't think He had the power to change me.
I did not believe.
I never thought I would find happiness
After all those times we were homeless.
Yes, sleeping in a train station.
Cause we couldn't afford to pay rent.
I remember this as if it were yesterday.

I was beaten all the time and sexually abused.
Always hearing the voice of Satan saying that I will always lose.
A girl that was always fighting.
My true emotions were always hiding.
The one that lost her daughter at the age of fourteen.
The one with no money.
Starving, always hungry.
Just to get by, I was always stealing.
Begging for healing.
Addicted to alcohol.
Dancing with demons after night fall.

Naked, clothes, I barely wore.
Carried myself like a whore.
I had no real relationships.

I just used both women and men.
After all I've gone through, do you really think I can trust them again?
Prostituting for money, drugs, and food while screaming Jesus's name.
Finding blood on my nose the next morning
From sniffing so much cocaine.
Oh, how I would've killed to do any drug, especially heroin.
Doing whatever Satan wanted while drinking and clubbing.
Arrested for defending myself from getting beaten.
I was such a despicable heathen.

Popping pills landed me in the hospital.
The attempt at suicide was once again not successful.
Intimacy with girls, thinking I'm bisexual.
Wandering the streets late at night, hopping from clubs to bars.
So bent, slowly killing myself, thinking I was on the planet Mars.
Smoked so much weed, I'd pass out.
Why the hell am I still living!
Is what I'd scream the next morning out loud.

Quick tempered, always lost control.
Spoke of Satan many times and ended up in a psych ward.
The school thought I was insane.
It was just foolish to think that God could take away my pain.
Couldn't go one sentence without a curse.
Didn't go one day without crying.
Never expressed how I truly felt except through my poetry writing.

I went for counseling, but it did not work.
Walked out of that office still feeling empty and hurt.
Loved the piercings, had messed up hair, and devilish eyes.
Yet, it still did not fill this emptiness no matter how hard I tried.
I was obsessed with needles.
Sick in the mind, not thinking right.

L.I.F.E.

Tried so many times to take my own life.
It became an obsession.
I desperately tried to escape the depression.
I would beat and cut myself up.
I bled so much when I tried to kill myself.
Rushed to the hospital again. I needed serious help!

I was so full of anger and hatred.
Yet used the ones I hated just to get wasted.
Voices in my mind.
Snorted so many lines.
I thought they would leave my head.
Daydreaming of my coffin bed.
I saw many demons and we conversed.
Not realizing what would come of it would be the worst.
I thought they were my best friends.
But now that I realize it,
They drove me to suicide and tried to bring my life to an end.

There is still so much more to say.
I went through so much at a young age.
If God can change me, then He can change you.
Just give your life to Him and watch what He will do.

December 18, 2000

How Could You Love Me?

How could You love me?
How could this be?
I will never understand.
Why did You take the nails from my hands?
Why did You take the beatings from my body?
Why didn't You just turn away and leave?
That whip should have been addressed to me.
I should have been the one to bleed.
I should be the one to burn in a pit.
Instead, my name is in the book of life on that list.
Why did You hang on that cross?
When I am the one who is at fault?
I cannot comprehend.
Lord, why did You send
Your Son to die for me?
How could You love someone like me?
I look in the mirror and say how could You save her?
I am a disgrace.
I always make mistakes.
I cursed You, Jesus!
I damned You, Jesus!
I hated You, oh, Lord Jesus!
But You still love me.
After all that I have done and went through
Lord, how could You say, *I still love you.*

L.I.F.E.

I just cannot see.
It is so hard to believe.
It is crazy to think that all that I have done was already paid for.
Someone else took on my death sentence.
You rose from the grave and defeated death.
Because of this, I will be with You forever in Heaven instead.
All You ask of me is to believe, repent, and sin no more.
How could You love me?
I know You do.
It's just hard to believe that You do.

January 30, 2001

Unforgettable

Mother's Day.
What a horrible day.
As the years go by,
I will not forget
About the one I love
But never met.
Just went up above,
As soon as you left.
Still holding my tummy as if you were there.
Reality is emptiness and it just isn't fair.
It kills to know that my love, I couldn't keep.
Everlasting punishment was the only thing left for me.
Oh daughter, after years, it still hurts!
I'd kill just to go back on my words.
Why can't I undo what has been done?
Why can't I change my actions just this once?
I don't care what people say, you are still alive!
In my heart, I still believe you did not die.
I don't care what people think, I am still a mom.
Even though I don't see you, I believe you are not gone!
Oh, what pain still exists!
What cries that drive away bliss.
Oh, why did you fly away?
Stay, why didn't you stay?
Mother's Day, what a horrible day!

March 12, 2001

Help Me to Remember

Troubles roll in.
Giving birth to sin.
I try to handle it by myself.
Forgetting my powerful Father that desires to help.
So, there I go.
Not remembering to be dependent.
But please know,
I do not wish You to be offended.
I don't purposely slip away.
From Your grace,
I don't mean to turn from Your face.
I have filth and shame in my life.
Not in Your presence,
Because I am not washed with the blood of Christ.
When You try to get near,
I run because I fear.
I seem to succeed in forgetting who You are.
My knowledge of Your love goes afar.
I am sorry that I doubt You, oh Lord.
Not remembering what Jesus died for.
Sometimes it's so difficult to believe
That Your love still lingers on to me.
Another like You,
I will never find.
My Prince of peace,
Help me to keep truth in mind.

April 27, 2001

You've Taught Me So Much

It's almost going to be one year
Since I've given my life to You.
Ever since You've been here,
Life has been so beautiful.
I've been seeing a lot of things differently.
Ever since You gave me sight,
I've been seeing things a whole lot clearly
Because now I see with light.
I've consented to acceptance.
I embrace the truth.
You've taught me how to have tolerance,
Especially towards the ones that speak against You.
I know how to love others.
It's all because of You.
And You're still giving me guidance,
The way no one has ever done or will do.
I'm learning not to hate.
I'm learning all things can be done by faith.
Whenever things don't go my way,
I am learning to lift my hands with joy and just pray.
You have given me an open mind
To understand why people are the way they are.
Even though I may not like it,
You showed me how to have a loving heart.
You taught me how to have patience.

L.I.F.E.

You've taught me obedience.
You've taught me honesty.
You've taught me that love is the key.
When I feel like giving up,
When life gets so tough,
You always show me that there is a way.
Comforting me, You always know what to say.
Life is difficult to deal with,
But You've made me strong.
I never thought I could handle it,
But You definitely proved me wrong.
You have taught me so much.
Ever since we've been together,
You've been an amazing Father.
In pursuit of me, thank you for sending my big brother!

May 27, 2001

Simply Beauty

My walks, my runs.
Ever since my life has begun.
The things that I find because of an open mind.
The courage to walk in the dark.
The lack of fear that is in my heart.
My experiences, what I have faced.
What I've seen, what I have tasted.
The struggles of life.
To get what I want,
I had to strive.
Every mark on me is a teacher.
Every injury holds a lesson.
If I don't become a keeper,
Then the advice won't release my tension.
All my cuts and all my bruises have a word it likes to mention.
My blood likes to speak.
My eyes reply with a weep.
My losses, my gains.
My heartaches and pain.
My strength that helps me to go on.
Love and truth keep me strong.
Out of agony comes knowledge.
Out of knowledge comes growth.
Even though my heart was countlessly damaged,
The true love given to me is all I need to know.

L.I.F.E.

The faith, the belief.
Everything inside of me,
Is simply beauty.

August 14, 2002

This Will Pass

Every face that I have encountered,
Every voice that I have spoken to,
I'll see and hear them all again.
They'll be called for their hearts to mend.
Every enemy will be sent to me
To hear His voice sing through me.
Awaiting and praying.
Weeping and praising.

It'll be on top of a mountain.
They'll be dying for thirst from His fountain.
Hunger for Him, they will feel.
Yearning to be healed. He will show them that He's real.
There will be a loud cry out into the heavens.
All hearts will be seeking Him, crying out repentance.

They'll surrender all and their souls will bow,
And then a mighty hand will descend from the clouds.
His spirit will flow through the air.
The power of it will be too much to bear.
A voice will spread through the sky.
The sin within will die.

A whisper echoes through the mountains,
Calling them to His throne.

L.I.F.E.

His words, spoken through my poetry,
Lead you all the way home.
He will grip you into His power
And never let you go.
He will take you into His arms.
Evil will lose its control.

They will see and feel Him in the wind.
They will be begging for forgiveness for all their sins.
They will see and feel Him in the sky.
They will lift His name on high.
He will be seen everywhere.
His cleansing blood is the clothes that they'll wear.

He will give them ears to hear.
A delivered message through the language of tongues.
Through my mouth, it'll be sung.
He will give them eyes to understand and see.
The truth that will be brought through me.

They will hear legions of angels sound their trumpets from above.
The people will be showered with His indefinite love.
This will happen; this will soon pass.
To breathe love and life into you that'll be so vast.
This is my vision.
This is my mission.
Just wait and see.
He will come for thee.

December 31, 2002

All For a Reason

I have another gift that I've yet to gain
Which is to speak and help the weak.
That is why I went through so much pain.
I see now that I was needing,
All the agony was for a meaning.
I was given the experience,
Given the knowledge for my purpose.
My destiny revealed through your encouraging verses.
Go into all the world and preach the gospel to all creation.[1]
My life's journey was for this intention.

God knew it was all for a reason.
The experience needed to be obtained.
So, whether it was sniffing a line of cocaine,
Or living in a poor broken home that made me go insane,
Or selling my body to the night,
For those five dollars in your pocket,
At that time, I was not meant to do right,
But it hurt Him just to watch it.

Every ache that I've felt through my adolescence,
Very young when I was stripped of my innocence,
It hurt my Lord to see,
But it'll all be worth it in the end is what He tells me.
Every single bruise

L.I.F.E.

Has been given to me to use.
It is all a testimony.
My life is proof that God is real.
That He has the power to heal.

I am a speaker, and I will help many others.
I will preach the Word to my sisters and brothers.
Every flame that has burned my skin
Is a mark to remind me of my sin,
A reminder of what I was delivered from.
The Lord has seen me through.
When I look back, I see where He has led me to.

Thank you, Lord, for letting me know the truth.
All that was done in my life is living proof.
Many will come forth for help,
But I know not to worry, for I will not be by myself.
Lord, speak for me.
Let my past be heard.
All hearts will be touched by Your words.
Many will relate to my past,
And see what You've done in my life.
Many will now see all that I have,
And that is the love and happiness in my life.
It was all for a reason.
It was all for the best.
It was all worth it.

January 5, 2003

Now Is the Time

You are no longer there but here.
I am told that my time is near.
I wish I could say that I'm not scared, but my heart isn't steady.
He's telling me that I must be ready.
My time has come
Where the Lord's will, through me, shall be done.
Even though I fear what is about to happen,
I know I will not be forsaken.
I know He will be there with me to the very end.
My life began with such unimaginable pain.
Now it will end with such happiness that I have gained.

You're slowly gaining control.
I feel it in my soul.
I feel you in my heart.
This is where the journey starts.
Through my arm, through my hand, straight to my fingertips,
You write such words that are so powerful that it hits.
Your words will be spoken
To the hearts of the broken.
All the words that I will recite,
You will bring it all to life.
From my heart, through my throat, right out of my mouth.
Such remarkable melodies that you will let out.

L.I.F.E.

Yes, the coming of Christ is almost here.
The Scriptures will come to pass. It shall all be done.
His victory has overcome.
He is calling out to His people,
Saying *do not listen to the deceitful*.
Songs, promises, love, a call.
With Your majestic voice, You will summon all.
The message, the domination, all that is written.
Such miracles that You'll do that it'll be hard not to believe in.

It is time to live up to what I was born for.
It is time to use the gifts given to me to serve the Lord.
I will grip my purpose, finally living up to what I'm destined to do.
To teach, speak, sing, bring the unbelievers to you.
Right before multitudes, I will lift my head towards the sky and sing.
Sending praises and worship to my King.
Throughout the entire world, the Word will spread.
His mighty power will wake the dead.

Use me, oh Lord.
I will surrender and do as you please.
I will be Your servant.
I will go into the world,
Leading the people into Your presence with my God-given gifts.
So, that you may revive and uplift.
Till the very end, I will fight the darkness
With the sword You have placed in my hands.
Use me to deliver them into the promised land.

January 5, 2003

You Gave Me Everything

I asked him a question.
He told me a lie.
I gave him my eyes.
He made me blind.
I gave him my ears.
He made me deaf.
I gave him my life.
He gave me death.
I gave him my heart.
He broke it into a thousand pieces.
I gave him my body.
He gave me destruction.
He raped and murdered me.

I gave You the lie.
You gave me the truth.
I gave You my blindness.
You gave me sight.
I gave You my deaf ears.
You gave me hearing.
I gave You my body.
You cleansed and healed me.
I gave You my heart.
You stitched it back together.
I gave You my destruction.

L.I.F.E.

You rebuilt me.
I gave You my emptiness.
You gave me peace.
You took my death and gave me Your life.

The more I think about this, I just don't understand.
I am blown away by this.
I cannot comprehend the vastness of Your love.
I gave You no time.
Paid You no mind.
I doubted You.
I did not believe in You,
Yet You were still there the whole time.
You never left my side.
Lie after lie, sin after sin.
And yet You still love me.
You were never ashamed of me.
You never gave up on me.
Oh Father, I don't know how to thank You.
No words can describe You and all You do.
You are an amazing Father.
You give me everything despite all that I have done.
I love You.

January 5, 2003

Home With You

I saw a road.
My curiosity emerged.
I was often told
To just stick to the one who I serve.
But again, not this time.
The Lord whispered
You've made a decision that was not mine.
As I was walking down this road,
It began to get dark and very cold.
I was isolated.
His guiding footsteps were no longer in my vision.
This slowly came to realization.
I wandered away from His side.
In Him, I no longer confide.
I felt cuts on my feet.
A trail of blood behind me.

I got lost.
Does He see that I'm not there?
Find me, for I am scared.
Shine your light,
So that I may find You.
Break this darkness,
So that I may get through.
Let me hear Your voice.

L.I.F.E.

Allow it to guide me out.
I'm sorry that I made the wrong choice.
I guess I have fallen again into doubt.

I want to come back home
Into Your arms, knowing that I'm not alone.
I want You, oh Lord.
I have no other desire.
I need You.
Your love that keeps me from burning in fire.
Your truth sets me free.
The miracle done in my life that keeps me to believe.
Such power that fills me up.
Your blood that cleans me up.
Each whip to Your flesh is my sin.
I still don't understand why you took it all in.
I can't believe how amazing You are.
It's Your love that keeps us from breaking apart.

Forgive me for going passed my boundary.
Thank you, Father, for having found me.
I was very foolish to roam.
I want to stay here with You at home.
Where I am loved, safe, and secure.
Home with You is where it all endures.
Thank you, Jesus.

January 15, 2003

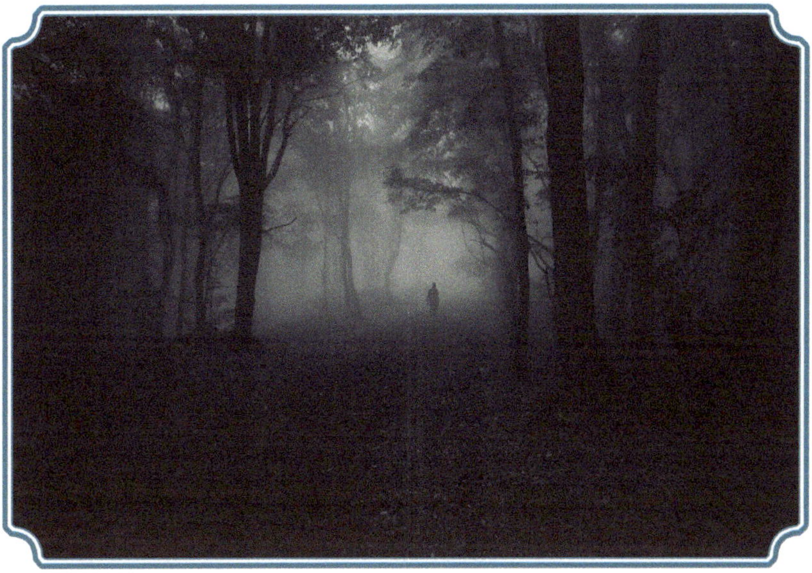

The Lost

Deep in the desert,
Hidden behind the winds of sand.
Trying to not be in the reach of man.
Underground homes,
Wanting your name and identity to be unknown.
In the woods, behind the trees.
Trying to use them as security.
They will try to escape the insanity.
In fear, so many will run.
Yes, the worst has yet to come.

Many will abandon their families just to hide.
They will turn from their own brothers just to save their own lives.
Parents will kill their own children.
Others will die by their own hands.
Many will give in to his command.
Many will fall into the night.
Due to their lack of faith, they will lose the fight.
Everything will be darkened; no light will shine.
Everything will fall; nothing will stand during this time.
Blood will be showered on this place.
Will you stand firm or fall away from your faith?
Hatred and chaos will bring forth war.
But who will you choose to stand for?
In these days, it'll be the most horror the world has ever seen.

Poor is the one that did not hear the call of the Messenger.
If they only believed in You.
If they only accepted the truth.
Such a cry throughout the world that has never been heard before.
Such pain that will be felt that will not be equal
To the pains of the beginning of time.
It'll be a hundred times worse than before.
They have no idea what lies before them.
What is yet to come is beyond their minds.
All this will happen in these very times.
They just won't believe their eyes when they see.
They will regret what they didn't believe.
I have sympathy for those that will be left behind.

At that very moment, when the clouds unfold,
The very sight of You, will shake their souls.
There will be no blindness.
Flesh will fall to the ground.
Who You are will be their confession.
You are the King of kings and Lord of lords.

February 17, 2003

Seeking You

My Lord,
I try to get to you.
Searching far, high, and low.
At night, I chase you in my dreams.
For reality is what it seemed.
I will search deep within a forest.
I will keep searching with no rest.
I'll go out into an open field and scream out Your name.
Run after You through the pouring rain.
I seek You through the night.
Searching for Your beautiful light.
Follow Your footsteps through the snow.
Father, lead me where I need to go.
Climb the highest mountain.
Then summon an eagle to jump on its back
And soar into the skies and search for You in the clouds.
Night falls, and then I search for You in the stars.

All I desire is You.
All I yearn for is You.
Let me run away with You.
I want to know everything about You.
I am dying of hunger and thirst for You.
I want more and more.
Tell me what it is I need to do, oh Lord.

Desiree Castillo

I don't care how long it takes.
I will find You.
I don't care how far I must go.
I will catch You.
I will search for You with all my heart, all my mind, and all my soul.
You are my true love.
In Your embrace is where my home is.
If anyone wishes to find me, they must search for You.
For where You are is where I'll be.

February 17, 2003

Leaving All For You

I look behind me.
I see all that is there.
Family, home, school.
I will leave it all behind me.
I must do this.
Right now is the time.
Not many will approve of this
But will understand later, all in due time.

You said that faith is dead without deeds.[2]
Without actions backing up my words, how can You work through me?
So, I have heard Your call, now my heart is listening.
I want to take this chance.
I will walk by faith.
My past, I have glanced.
All of it was done for my fate.

I don't know what lies ahead.
But I remember in the Scriptures that You said,
I am with you always, even to the end of the age.[3]
So, I am willing to drop all and believe what You say.
I know that I will suffer,
But I will go all the way.

Desiree Castillo

Knowing that I will be persecuted
Because of Your name.
I know that I will be hated,
Yet I will never stop loving You.
I will pick up my cross and follow You.
Into war, into pain, into distress, into all that lies ahead.
I will follow You until the very end.

Lord, please give me the strength to keep moving on and not look back.
Place the Holy Spirit in me to defeat the enemy.
Help me to overcome those that block the way in my path
And for them to not take away the purpose that I have.
Give me spiritual eyes to see nothing but the truth,
Spiritual ears to hear only Your voice.
Where will You lead me, where will I go?
What is my destination?
I trust You will show me how.
You didn't bring me this far to leave me now.

Father, let my heart speak to You.
I want my voice to reach up to Your throne,
My words to reach Your ears.
I pray that at night, an angel will take this letter,
And deliver this message to You.
To the heavens, my words will fly.
Let what I write be seen by Your fiery eyes.
Read this, hear what I say, and feel what I feel for You.
That is the love that I have for You.

February 17, 2003

All I've Ever Wanted

All I've ever wanted,
I wanted from the ones that I loved.
Since I was a little girl,
I longed to be loved.
All I wanted was to be wanted.
Just wanted to be held tight by my mother.
Sought for a hug from my father.
Longed for a true kiss from a lover.
Whenever I was injured, I wanted someone to run to my aid.
Whenever I cried, I wanted someone to wipe my tears away.
I wanted someone to play with.
Someone to talk to.
Oh, how I searched long for it.
I wanted to be desired.
I wished for someone to search me.
To look for my smile.
For someone to run after me.
All I wanted was love,
Yet I never found it.
I wanted to be someone to somebody.
I wanted my name to be called from someone else's mouth.
My voice to be heard from an ear.
All my life while growing up, I have wanted this.
But it wasn't there.
I wanted a true home.
But instead, I was alone.

So, I continued to search in circles.
Searched in different places.
Traveled the world but nothing there.
Many people came in and out of my life and yet still nothing there.
But one day I turned to the next person in search of love.
And I saw a stranger with His arms open.
I looked at Him and stared and just stared.

Since you were in your mother's womb,
I've been watching you.
I've been following you everywhere.
I was there while you were growing up.
I heard all your cries.
When you thought you were alone, I was there.
I listened to everything you have said.
Was even there when you were sleeping in bed.
I watched everything you did.
I was there before you even got injured, when you got hurt.
I was there when you sang, there when you wrote.
I was always there by your side.
There with you when you went through all in your life.
I heard and felt your desire for love.
And so, I am here to answer your call.
I am love. Love is my name.

He revealed Himself to me.
At that moment, I fell into His arms.
This is my true family.
He is the one that feeds me.
Talks to me.
Hugs, holds, and kisses me.
This stranger took me in.
I was dirty, sinful, not to be trusted, and all alone,

L.I.F.E.

But He took me into His home.
Everything He has I want.
He came to me with truth, life, but most of all, love.

February 18, 2003

I Won't Give Up

You warned me about this.
You warned me about them.
Since I was born,
Many looked down on me.
My own family would turn on me,
And say that I wouldn't make it.
They would say I don't know what I am doing or where I am going.
But Lord, how many times have You proved them wrong?
And yet they still don't believe in You.
I know that what I am trying to achieve is impossible with man
But possible with You.
That is why I put all my trust in You.
You told me that the cost of following You is a lot.
What I will face deals with great pain.
Regardless of all the pain I must endure,
Or how many put me down,
I will make it in the name of the Lord.
It was not easy to leave it all for You,
But that's what I wanted to do.
All I want is You.
You are my guidance.
My light in darkness.
My education, my Teacher.
My food and drink.
You will be my shelter all the way.

L.I.F.E.

My armor till the end.
I will not worry and keep looking up.
I fix my eyes on You.
Your will be done.

February 19, 2003

To The Unwise

Very foolish you are.
Yes Lord, forgive them for they know not what they do.
Your ears pick up a different message from the lips.
You are quickly aggressive to put up your fist.
You hear one thing and interpret it differently to another.
You foolishly let Satan get between you and your brother.

Listen to yourself.
Hear your own tongue deceive.
You need serious help.
Only the Lord can help you not to believe.
Never have I turned against you.
None of these quarrels would have happened
If you had considered the truth.

I rebuke you, evil spirit!
And as for you, let your ears not hear it!
You turn against me as if I am the enemy.
But the true enemy is the invisible that lies before your face.
It's absurd and I pity the things you do.
Nevertheless, I still have love for you.

February 28, 2003

Slowly Awakening

He was asleep, awakening slowly.
He is already here, but he isn't known yet totally.
His being is so horrible to even tell.
His footsteps leave a trail of worms from Hell.
His heart is black.
He breathes fire.
His eyes are empty.
His body is hard and very cold.
His smell is of burning coal.
Now he breathes. He walks.
You'll be lured by his talks.
He is already making sense to some.
From the truth, ears have turned numb.
He hasn't made his appearance known.
But he will soon be fully grown.
For it's not his time yet.
He and the words of the book have not met.

Right now, he is watching and waiting.
Watching the world fall into a trap.
His purpose is still until that.
The people will call for a savior.
He will make sure that he will be the one they favor.
Then he will slither his way in.
When the world expects his arrival,

He will be the one they'll call reliable.
His voice will be hidden with a mask.
To deceive you into the dark is his task.
His voice will hypnotize.
Then his authority will rise.
He will enforce many laws that he'll make.
He will claim you with a mark that you'll have to take.
If you were wise, you'd be alive.
Before all this, you would have been taken away.
Such times will be so bad.
The people will feel as if he is all they have.

So true he will sound to your hearing.
So pleasing and comforting to your heart.
You'll feel as if you want to turn to him for everything,
And then you'll refuse to ever be apart.
The wonders from his very fingers,
Will give you more of a reason to linger.
He will be so clever, so sly.
He will even get many believers to deny.
Many will look up to him as a hero.
He intends to bring all to place a million degrees above zero.

If you are saved, you have nothing to fear.
So be ready, for His coming is very near.
You surely do not want to see what will be done.
Make sure your name is written,
So that you may be taken when He comes.
Accept the ever-lasting love of integrity He has for you.
Living the holy life is what you must do.
He won't be silent for long.
So, ask the Almighty to forgive you for all the sins you've done.

L.I.F.E.

Time has been shortened.
Days are passing quickly.
The time is near when all must take place.
Be ready.

March 7, 2003

My Angelina

I have a new life now with my little companion.
A new beginning, a fresh start.
The moment you were born, I looked upon your face,
And you stole my heart.

You make me so happy.
This joy makes me cry.
The way you make me feel, I truly can't describe.

I thank the Lord for you every day.
I did not deserve to be blessed in this way.
After the way I treated you Lord,
I shouldn't have been given this.
Yet You blessed me with such eternal bliss.

You gave me her.
Overtaken, now I'm captured.
The impossible happened.
I have fallen deeply in love,
With an angel that was sent from above.

She has made me whole, made me complete.
The smallest person in the world has conquered me.
I just can't believe she is mine.
She is truly a God-sent.

L.I.F.E.

She is my heart, my queen, my precious, my treasure.
I just can't imagine my life without her.

I promise you that you will not suffer as I did.
I promise you will not go through what I've been through.
I will always be here for you
To protect you, support, and love you unconditionally.

I will guide you
Not only as your mother but as your best friend.
We'll always be together till the very end.
I am no longer alone in this world.
We are now a small family of two.
My Querida, I love you.

April 30, 2004

Dear Mother

We don't really speak.
I don't know you.
You don't know me.
We are strangers.
Your neglect, put us through a lot of danger.
I always longed for you, though.
Desired the warmth of a mother.
I always longed for your embrace.
Yet you always made me feel like I was a disgrace.
I wish I knew what it was like to have a relationship with you.
Because of your abandonment,
Love in all the wrong areas is what I pursued.
I never even heard you say you love me.
But out of everything,
The pain, the suffering,
The physical abuse, the neglect,
All the times I felt the reject,
Being homeless on the streets,
After what you let him do to me,
I forgive you.
Although many years were lost,
We will be together hand in hand one day.
Memories of the past will fade away.
I will hold you so tight, both of our hearts will beat as one.
Sorrows of the past will be undone.

L.I.F.E.

I will whisper that I love you and believe you will do the same.
We will walk in the Kingdom of Heaven together,
And spend eternity getting to know each other.
I'm sorry for any pain I caused you.
Know that I have always longed for and loved you.

January 26, 2008

The Night I Met You

I remember the night I first met You.
Eight years ago.
A moment that was so powerful.
We were all in a circle.
Surrounding the fire.
In the middle of the woods.
I was singing so loudly that the angels looked down from Heaven.
I was crying out to You. I gave in!
I looked straight into the flames and told You my heart's desire.
I surrendered.
I put it all on the cross.
You appeared.
I saw You in that fire.
I saw Your eyes.
No earthly words can truly describe.
Such beauty.

It glowed like diamonds.
So bright, so warm, so loving.
I had never seen such beauty before.
You took me as I was.
I saw these arms open and embraced me.
I saw You there.
In the fire!
Couldn't believe what I was seeing.
Couldn't believe or understand what I was feeling.
Your presence strongly filled that place.
I heard the trumpets.
I heard the angels praising You.
I felt them drop to their knees and bow.
The earth trembled.
The trees shook.
I heard Your footsteps.
You came to me.
The third of the trinity.
Filled me with You.
You broke the chains off my ankles and wrist.
I bathed in Your blood that night.
You saved me.
I became born-again.

January 28, 2008

My Image

Father, it is amazing that I can even call You Dad.
It gives me such great joy to know what I have.
God is my Father, so that makes me a queen!
I own more than I can possibly imagine in my wildest dreams.
You have placed a crown on my head.
I am rich, have dominion and authority, according to what You said.
It is amazing that I was made in Your image and likeness.
I look like You! To look like the one and only true God, what beauty!
You have given me immortal eyes to see past worldly things.
You have given me wisdom to conquer this world victoriously.
The blood that I was bought with runs through my veins.
Because of Your love, I have a different last name.
I was adopted into Your wonderful family.
You bless me abundantly.
I can go boldly to Your throne and ask for anything.
I can go boldly to Your throne to praise and sing.
There I am, before Your presence in the heavens.
I am in Your throne room, giving You reverence
In front of a host of angels.
I love to put a smile on Your face.
I know You are pleased because I feel Your warm embrace.
You made me ruler of this earth.
You have clothed me with royalty since birth.
Anyone that tries to harm me, You put them below my feet.
If You are for me, then who can be against me?

L.I.F.E.

Even the demons tremble at my sight.
Once they see You in me, they don't dare put up a fight!
Now I know they are more afraid of me then I of them,
Because You have given me dominion.
I know who I am. I am the daughter of the one and only true God.
My brother is Jesus, so that makes me the sister of a King.
Because of this knowledge, I will forever be rejoicing!

September 28, 2008

I Am Sorry

I have displeased You. I have disobeyed You.
There is no explanation that I can give You.
Forgive me, but my heart is curious.
I am truly sorry if I made You furious.
I did not mean to hurt You or cause You any pain.
I cannot point fingers at the devil, for I am the one to blame.
I still love You. I love You so much.
My fleshy desires do not give me an excuse to touch.
I have no right, for my body does not belong to me.
He claimed it the very moment He died for me.
It was bought at a great price on that cross.
Free me from this bondage that is even burned in my thoughts.
I have turned my back on You once for another.
I refuse to do that again.
I will not leave the arms of my Father.
Please help me to not give birth to sin!
I'd rather lose all than to lose You.
I cannot bear it.
I'm so scared of losing You again.
Please forgive my acts and thoughts.
I shouldn't have strayed from what I was taught.
How could I have let them play these tricks?
Only Your strength can get me through because alone, I can't resist.
What can I say, my Lord?
Losing my robe of righteousness is what I can't afford.

L.I.F.E.

Show me Your ways. Help me to live holy before Your eyes.
I want to be highly favored and pleasing before Your sight.
Have mercy, oh God. Do not turn Your face.
Although I am not worthy, do not see me as a disgrace.
I beg You, my love! I am on my knees.
I cry out, Father, have mercy on me.
I was wrong, and I cannot reverse what has been done.
You are the center of my heart; You are the only one!
What can I do?
What can I say?
I am sorry, and I love You.

October 4, 2008

You Know

You know me better than I know myself.
You know the situation better than I do.
I can't get through this without Your help,
But I find it so hard to be patient with You.
I find myself trying to figure You out.
Wondering what this is all about.
Why must I suffer so? I'm in a great deal of pain.
Yet this is something You already know
Because out of this trial comes great gain.
You know the depth that I am in.
You know the thoughts in my mind.
I am weighed down with such a heavy burden.
I feel like I'm in a bind.
You see these chains tight upon my neck.
Trying to catch one breath.
Set me free.
Give me peace.
Your Word says *blessed is the one who goes through trials.*[4]
Blessings will come through.
You discipline the ones You love,[5]
To get to that next level with you.
You ask me to just be still and know that You are God.[6]
Why am I finding this hard to do?
Patience is so difficult to endure.
I just can't wait anymore.

L.I.F.E.

Help me, oh God, please set me free!
Faith is now; help me to just know.
You know how this is going to turn out.
You have my best interest at heart.
Your timing is perfect.
In this storm, I'm supposed to let You do Your job.
All I need to do is be still and know that You are God!

October 13, 2008

Inside

I saw her.
She was looking in a mirror, so hideous beyond imagination.
Her face was unbearable to look at.
It was deformed, burned, and ugly.

I saw her sitting there, all alone in the restaurant,
Holding a glass of wine.
She was looking down at her own reflection in her drink.
She was despising her face.
No one would look her way.
No one would approach her.
She wouldn't even get a friendly hello.

There she was, back in front of that mirror.
She doesn't possess any beauty.
She cannot meet the expectations of another.
She took a knife, put it right to her chest above her breast,
And she pressed against her body as hard as she could.
Then she dragged the knife downward, all the way to her belly button.
She slit her body open in half.

She couldn't believe what she found inside of herself.
Such beauty no words can describe.
It was unbelievable.
It was priceless.

More valuable than any materialistic thing in the world.
Richer than money or jewels.
What was in her, most of the world did not possess.

You dwelled in her.
You made her Your home.
God built a kingdom inside her.
You dressed her and filled her with treasures, knowledge, and wisdom.
The sweet aroma that came from her insides!
Such vibrant colors that shined from within her!
Despite what she looked like on the outside,
I just couldn't believe what I saw inside of her.

With a smile on her face, she took a needle with some thread
And stitched herself back up slowly.
She looked in the mirror.
She didn't see the burns.
Her face was not deformed.
It was simply wool over her eyes that deceived her into believing that.
She was the most beautiful woman I have ever seen.
No voluptuous woman in the world could compare
To what she was and what she had.
She possessed something greater than a lustful body.
She had power, authority, wisdom, and knowledge
That was far beyond the comprehension of this world.
She is immortal because of You!
This is me.

March 15, 2010.

Do You Really Think I Don't Know?

You feel as if you are all alone in this world.
You feel that no one understands your pain.
You have been abused.
Abandoned.
No one to turn to. No one to talk to.
Ridiculed and mocked.
Do you think all of this is far beyond my comprehension?
Try me.
Who knows suffering and loneliness more than I?
Did I not leave my throne and come in human form?
Have I not walked in this world before you?
I faced many oppositions.
Trials and temptations.
I have walked on dangerous grounds.
I have felt extreme anxiety. I begged for the cup to be taken from me.
In that hour, I was abandoned by all who followed me.
I was denied.
In the very last hour, I was abused, beaten.
I was killed for something I did not do
Yet chose to lay down my life for you.
You had no idea what I had to endure
So don't tell me I don't know or don't understand.
Because I do!
I completely understand how you feel.
I can relate to what you are going through.

L.I.F.E.

I've been there.
Come to me, and I will heal you.
Come to me, I will give you peace.
Desirée, you will cry no more.
Nothing is too great for me.
All your pain, all your suffering, every problem must kneel to my name.
I have already conquered this world, so there is nothing I can't handle.
You never have to face this world alone. I made a promise to you.
Trust me.
I am with you. I will always be with you.

December 29, 2010

My Shepherd Comes for Me

My Lord, I do not hear Your voice.
Have I gone deaf?
Has Your Spirit left?
I open the book and see a blank page.
War, he continues to wage.

There is another that calls out to me.
Such a familiar voice.
I recognize this voice from long ago.
Instead of saying no,
I made the wrong choice.
I followed the whispers.
I waltzed into the night.
I slow danced with darkness.

Why do you keep me so close to you?
What is it about me that disturbs you?
What do you know that I don't know?
You have haunted me since birth.
Is the pursuit of me really of great worth?
His calling on my life must be huge!
To let me go, you refuse.

L.I.F.E.

You have a tight grip on my neck.
I can barely breathe.
However, I feel a disconnect
As He removes your grip from me.
That beautiful light
Followed me into the night
To break up this slow dance
And to remind you of where you stand!

He follows me wherever I go,
Even when I was His foe.
No matter how many times I leave,
He will keep fighting you for me.
This sheep may have wandered away.
But look, my Shepherd comes for me.
The Lion of Judah will never leave me astray.

July 23, 2011

Show Yourself

Why did You really let it come to this?
I have lost everything.
A single mother struggling to make ends meet.
Working two jobs just so my baby can eat.
I have thirty-four cents to my name!
Merciful God, where are You?
I know You are real, so help me!
I am struggling.
I am suffering.
Show Yourself!
Do I really serve a lifeless God?
What have I done to allow this to come this far?
In the midst of it all, I am still alone!
Where is he, the one You promised me?
Why would You make me suffer?
The very thing I hate, You make me face!
Why are You doing this?
Where are the promises?
Where are the blessings?
Where is the breakthrough?
For years, I have called You for help.
Yet You ignored my prayers.
I can't do this by myself!
My own Father has given up on me.
I have tithed.

L.I.F.E.

I have been obedient.
I have served.
I don't know what else to do.
I'm tired. So tired. Burnt out!
I am facing what I have greatly feared.
I am alone.
My God has truly given up on me.
I don't blame Him.
I don't blame You for leaving me.

August 13, 2012

You Came to Me

Angelina saw You.
She told me this morning.
She did not know that for me; it was a night full of mourning.
Yet, she saw it all as she slept.
She saw You at the edge of my bed.
She trembled at the sight of You.
She cried to me as she was attempting to describe You.
Big, beautiful and very bright,
Is what my eight-year-old said she saw last night!
So, You actually came to me?
I poured my heart out to You.
I screamed. I shouted.
Of all Your promises, I doubted.
Despite all the hurtful words I said,
You still showed up at the edge of my bed.
You endured my painful words,
And then stayed the night with me.
She saw all this while asleep.
I don't deserve this after all that I said to You.
Yet, You never stop showing Your love for me no matter what I do.
Thank You for not leaving my side.
The confirmation came through her eyes.
I wish I could've been the one to see You.
Regardless, I am so grateful.

August 14, 2012

Time

You robber. You thief.
You are so beautiful.
Priceless, yet you steal.
You take without permission.
You don't need to.
You answer to no one.
You are so precious.
Each moment with you, no words can describe.
Each moment with you makes me wonder.
You make me ask myself, what am I doing?
What have I done?
You challenge me.
Your voice are the memories I hold.
Your voice are the pictures I see.
Your voice is the wrinkle on my face,
The strand of white that I find.
You are a gift that can't be bought.
Yet you take back what you give.
Your gift is temporal.
You robber! Beautiful thief!
Teach me how to use you.
What do I do with you?
In my death, many will speak of what I have done with you.
Everything about me will be told by you.
You give.

Desiree Castillo

You take.
That is what is so beautiful about you.
So many of us take you for granted.
What do I do with you, beautiful?
Laugh, dance, serve, give thanks to God!
There is much to do before you go.
You will never tell me when you'll be leaving me.
In my death, all will know what I have done with you.
In my death, your voice bears witness to what I have done for Him.
You beautiful, precious, priceless thief.

December 16, 2016

The Most Powerful Thing in The World.

I don't know you.
The only truth to you is the man that revealed you on the cross.
I only know of you on the third day.
The day of resurrection or even the day He was born.
I know nothing else about you, and I don't care to know.
I hold on to the one truth about you: Jesus laid his life for me.
You only exist because of Him.
Because of His actions.
No one else knows how to express you because
You don't exist in any other way.
I don't know you!
You end at the cross.
That is where your boundaries lie.
Without Him, you are nothing.
My only desire is to accept you through Him.
Other than this, stay away!
Stay far away!
You are not real!
I don't trust you!
I don't like you!
I don't care to know you!

December 16, 2016

The Wait Is Over

I honestly didn't think God would keep His promise.
Yet, He continued to insist
That I be still and wait.
But I had moments where I almost lost faith.
But now you are finally here
After waiting for sixteen years.
You are beyond my expectations.
You are far more beautiful than I imagined.
And the way you treat me, I never thought this could happen.
I never thought I could experience true love like this.
Everything about our relationship is so effortless.
He made you specifically for me.
He made me specifically for you.
This is ordained by Him.
My soul mate, my lover, my best friend,
Jonathan, you were worth the wait.

April 14, 2020

Father

Screams.
Screaming in my sleep.
Screaming in my dreams.
Countless days, I wake up screaming.
Visions of you.
Memories of the past.
Why couldn't the time last?

Walking down the hallway.
The scent of death everywhere.
Walking past body after body.
Darkness and defeat surround me.

I see you lying there.
I feel so helpless.
I wish I could've done something.
I couldn't touch you.
I couldn't hug you.
Couldn't be by your side.
A glass separated us, forbidding me to say goodbye.
How can they ask, *if his heart stops, do we resuscitate?*
Was my response truly a lack of faith?

Begged and pleaded with God for your life!
Day after day I mourned and prayed for more time.
Yet He told me, *He belongs to me! He is mine!*

I didn't want to accept this.
Regardless of knowing you were His.
Yet, I knew you were already gone way before that plug was pulled.
Believing made me feel like such a fool!

You appeared to me in my dreams, ignoring my indescribable pain.
Your only purpose in appearing was to repeatedly say His name.
Yes, I know where you are. I know who you're with!
I miss you, though, despite all this!
Your voice, your support, your love.
Yet I know you have a new eternal assignment from above.
Losing you was an unexpected severe blow.
But I know, I must let go.

What I have learned from you is humbleness and perseverance in the faith.
Now I take the baton you left behind and continue this race.
I will get as many souls as I can to Christ.
Thank you for setting that example in your life.
I love you, Father.
I will see you again.

2021

See You Again

Just one glance at it and you left.
You did not hesitate to take your last breath.
How cruel can time be to take you away from me?
In faith, I pondered.
Yet you couldn't just wait a little longer?

If you only knew my suffering, you would know why I left.
My healing and escape were in death.
Yes, I took one glance at it and did not turn back.
I could no longer put on a façade, years of a painful act.
Yet none of this changes what I feel for you.

It is not fair. You promised me more time.
This sudden escape brutally tortured my mind.
The least you could have done is say goodbye.
Sorry, but I would rather you live the lie.
I really miss you.

I did not say goodbye because I will see you again.
Forgive me, but I did not mean to offend.
I am in a much better place.
Trust me when I say you will once again feel my warm embrace.
To find me, wait to be put to the ground,
Then just follow the piano sound.

May 5, 2022

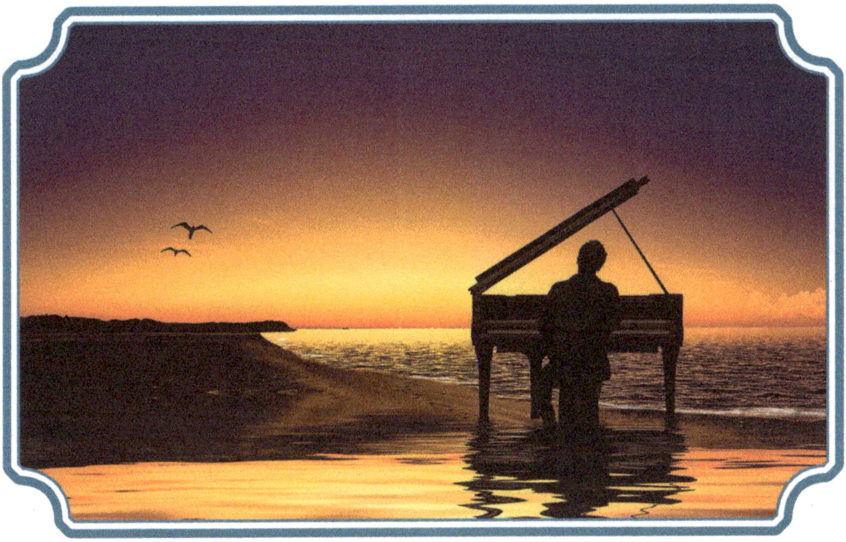

Not Again

How could this have happened?
Is this punishment for the murder I committed twenty-four years ago?
Answer me, Lord! Where is Your compassion!?
You, who parted the seas!
Because of You, she no longer bleeds!
You, who miraculously healed the sick!
She conceived yet never consummated!
Isn't this the power of the Holy Spirit?
Didn't You walk on water?
But to help me, You didn't even bother.
You raised the dead! Yet You couldn't raise mine!
How could You take their sibling away?! Her twin?!
Have I offended You? Reveal to me my sin.
What an image burned in my mind.
A lifeless body in me.
How could You allow this in my sight.
You could've brought him back with all Your might!
I see you, baby! Hear your mommy's voice.
Come back to me.
Let me hear your heartbeat!
Breathe, please, breathe!
I spoke over his body.
I sang to him. I spoke Your promises over him and yet You take him.
I feel broken.
I don't understand.

Why?
Answer me!
Why are You silent, my God?
How could You do this to me?
I believe You can do anything!
I believe in Your Word, Your power.
I believe You can do the impossible.
I know what You can do. I believed in every word You said.
I know You have the power to bring him back from the dead.
I am here, in Your throne room, at Your feet.
Pleading and begging You to give him back to me.
Not again, how could this have happened again?

July 2022

Silent

I've been silent for so long.
Stopped writing to pursue what was wrong.
How did he creep into the church? I failed to see.
How did his teachings change the Word
To motivational speeches of self-prosperity?
Baal entered because your spirit was missing to discern.
Many have fallen away to his concerns.
But the scales have finally come off my eyes.
Sanctified by the truth has made me wise.
I repent of my lust for money, status, and title.
My salvation and relationship with You are far more vital.
I have awakened. No longer under his spell.
I will no longer be silent. I will intercede for those blinded by his veil.
I am back, waging war.
I am coming after you with the lion of Judah's roar!

July 24, 2023

Awaken and Repent

Did He not warn of the yeast of the Sadducees and Pharisees?[7]
Because of their false teachings,
The churches are occupied by demonic deities.
The church is under attack by a beast.
Because they have absorbed the wrong yeast.

You had the audacity to alter the gospel!
Watering it down because you assume it is hostile.
Your so-called sermons are taught with silly props
To emotionally move the congregation.
Not realizing that you have given a front row seat to Satan.

You were to operate in the power and fire of the Holy Spirit.
But because you dismissed Him, you and the flock have become wicked.
You have turned the Word into "How To" motivational speeches
To gain possessions.
When you were told to heal the sick, cast out demons
And to preach repentance. [8]

You were to make more disciples![9]
Yet you preach the doctrines of Baal and turned away from the true gospel.
You were to operate with the gifts of the spirit spoken of in 1 Corinthians 12.
Yet you teach the flock to focus on themselves.

Pride in achievements and possessions is not from the Father. [10]
You were to teach about spiritual warfare and to put on the armor. [11]
You have made the house of prayer
Into a money-making entertainment venue.
If only He was here, He would flip the tables and condemn you.

How dare you teach five steps on "How To" gain status,
Titles, and achievements
When the core of the gospel is about salvation and repentance!
Did He preach on "How To" get a Louis Vuitton bag
Or "How To" get a promotion?
Oh, how the church became content and swallowed this yeast of poison!

Jesus did not preach this way.
What a heavy price He paid.
To the leaders of the church, repent of these teachings.
Surrender to the Holy Spirit and allow Him to do the preachings.
Do not be lukewarm and compromise. [12]
Awaken and turn to Christ.

July 29, 2023

The Body of Christ

3am.
Reiterating again.
You have awakened me at this hour for years.
However, I ignored it because I had no fear.
Audibly, I heard You say, *read Jeremiah 2:19*.
This was about me and the body of Christ backsliding.
A vision.
A pair of eyes.
Roaming the church.
What a reputation of lies.
You allowed me to see what You see.
So much darkness in the so-called house of the Lord.
The facade before You are what You abhor.
Sin runs wild among the flock.
Did we really think God can be mocked?[13]
There is no awe of You.
You allowed me to feel Your pain.
Immensely hurt and angry You are, I am unable to explain.
Because we have backslid so far!
Condoning sin, oh, how we believed the enemy's lies!
Starting with leadership, we live a compromised Christian life.
We have walked away from the true gospel, repentance.[14]
If we do not turn back, wrath will come with such vengeance.
We forsook You and Your Word.
I am so sorry, my Lord. Forgive me and the herd!

Turn back to Christ. Repent!
This is the true gospel and why He was sent!
Surrender to the Holy Spirit, for time is running out.
Have your oil lamps filled or you will be left out.[15]
We thought we were saved, but we're not.
Repent. Be ready before He knocks!

August 6, 2023

Shadows of My Past

I did not want to return here.
A dreadful time of pain and fear.
I was so young.
Not understanding what was happening.
Just wanted to play with my toys.
Just wanted to watch cartoons.
Little did I know I would grow up too soon.

His force, his touch, his embrace.
Disgusted by the way he tastes.
He hurt me again and again.
My innocence taken.
Oh, how I wish you would have saved me,
But instead, you watched.
Left me in shock.

So frightened to go to sleep.
So frightened to be alone with him.
Frightened to even speak.
Such evil, so prevalent.
With all their might, not even God's warring angels could stop this.
The falling ones joined him in the torment and abuse.
Year after year, I was used.
In his absence, they took his place.
Many nights, I was raped.

L.I.F.E.

But now, He has intervened and destroyed them completely.
By the power of the living God,
I have broken the ties.
I can now look you both in the eyes,
And say,
I forgive you.

September 1, 2023

YOU vs ME

How many take you so lightly?
You are barely spoken of, yet you are mentioned many times in the book.
It is no coincidence that you are mentioned in the first commandment.[16]
Oh, how this is so overlooked.
Your spells, your incantations.
Your possession, your influences.
Deceitful persuasions.

You disguise.
Superior intelligence, extremely wise.
So patient.
Luring the chosen to become complacent.

You study
To learn weaknesses.
Each with a special skill.
Conjure tactical plans to kill.
You are powerful, full of evil.
So cunning, so deceitful.

But

There is One more powerful than you.
You tremble at His presence.
Legions gather because they foolishly think they can take on the One.

L.I.F.E.

Have you not read what He has done?
Oh, wait!
You were there!
He took you out each time, even though you did not play fair.

I am a threat to you because He dwells inside of me.
I know the authoritative power I walk in.
I am aware of the weapons He gave me.

The Word.
So powerful.
Spoken and cherubim emerge,
By my side with their flaming swords.
Attempt to come near and you will be torn.

The Word.
When spoken it is manifested in the spiritual realm.
It is ammunition to bring you to submission.

The blood.
Oh, how you cannot stand the fragrance.
Drenched all over me.
For you, this is a major deterrence.
Just one sniff, one look at the blood,
And you must passover.
It is a shield. Protection.
Yet another powerful weapon.

His name.
You must bow to it.
Just a whisper and it disperses missiles.
Sending you back to the abyssal.

Desiree Castillo

I know the law, and I know you know it.
I know how to use this against you.
You come at me with your wicked schemes.
Expecting me to run, hide, and scream.
Yet I caught you by surprise with my offense attacks.
I know who lives inside of me, who goes before me, and who has my back.
You have no chance against me.

September 6, 2023

Does It Really Matter?

The money.
The success.
The titles.
Worldly possessions.
Not just in the world, but in the church, this is so heavily mentioned.
Does this really matter?
Climbing the corporate ladder?
You will never be successful without a degree.
I have heard this lie countlessly.
Is this all true?
You are nothing if you don't go to college.
In some ways this can open the door to bondage.
The focus will be on becoming successful.
The obsession will lead to burn out.
Is all of this what life is really about?
With all of the prosperity and money,
Why do I still feel empty?
In the end, when I am before Your throne
On judgement day, is this what will matter to you?
The one true living God?
Will getting a degree and becoming successful with a fancy title
Really matter to you?
No.

Many of us ask the question, *What is my purpose in life?*
Yet You gave us the answer already.
Go into all the world, preach the gospel, and make more disciples.[17]
This is everyone's purpose and calling.
The only difference is the method on how it is done.
The perfect example of what we are meant to do is in Your Son.
He lived a humble life and did Your will.
This is what matters.
This is what You will judge us on.
Not on the things of this world.

October 28, 2023

Call to Fight Back

Aren't you tired?
Blow after blow.
Beaten, attacked, mocked.
Don't you know?
Can't you discern the spirits?
No, because you are so far away from the ultimate Spirit.
You foolishly think he does not influence or tempt.
If he tempted the very Son of God,[18]
What makes you think you are exempt?
You are in combat!
So, put on your armor and fight back!
Blow after blow, the body of Christ endures.
Yet He trained us all for war!
That realm is real. Your opponent is real.
Wake up! Stop going by emotions and what you feel.
Go by the truth, facts, His Word!
What we cannot see is far more real than this world.
You have the power to move things in the spiritual realm.
Use the weapons He gave you.
You have the authority to overcome all the power of the enemy.[19]
He fights dirty, so don't wait to counterattack.
Don't wait to defend. Strike first. Fight back!
Don't sit idle any longer.
You are far more stronger.
You have the greatest army behind you.

Desiree Castillo

The greatest Commander before you.
Fight back! Enough is enough!

November 4, 2023

This Journey

This is for the reader of my poetry.
I write because I want to share the love that got a hold of me.
I may not be proud of the things I have done.
I have made countless mistakes and was always on the run.
This journey was not easy.
It isn't for anyone.
In life, you will venture through many obstacles.
You will take dark paths through moments of struggles.
You will also see glorious views while travelling through serene valleys.
As you can see in my writing, I have ignored many stop signs
And ended up in dark alleys.
No matter what, though, you are not alone.
My testimony is evident of this love shown.
He is alive. He is real. His name is Jesus.
I did not believe in Him at one point in my life.
Instead, the things of this world are what I strived.
But after experiencing everything the world has to offer,
I still felt so empty.
Despite feeling this, I ran away from Him countlessly.
I ended up on a dead-end street.
Face-to-face, there, He met me.
He desires to meet you, too.
He is madly in love with you.
That is why He laid down his life.
What He offers, no earthly words can describe.

Desiree Castillo

You have absolutely nothing to lose.
Give Him a chance. Do not delay.
His return is very soon.

November 17, 2023

Endnotes

1. Mark 16:15 NIV
2. James 2:17 NKJV
3. Matthew 28:20 NKJV
4. James 1:12 NIV
5. Hebrews 12:6 NIV
6. Psalms 46:10 NIV
7. Matthew 16:5-12 NIV
8. Mark 6:12-13 NIV
9. Matthew 28:19 NIV
10. 1 John 2:16 NLT
11. Ephesians 6:10-17 NIV
12. Revelation 3:15-16 NIV
13. Galatians 6:7 NIV
14. Matthew 4:17 NIV
15. Matthew 25:1-13 NIV
16. Deuteronomy 5:7 NIV
17. Matthew 28:19 NIV
18. Matthew 4:1-11 NIV
19. Luke 10:19 NIV